Grade 1

Carson-Dellosa Publishing LLC
Greensboro, North Carolina

Credits

Content Editor: Jeanette Moore, MS Ed.

Copy Editor: Angela Triplett

Visit *carsondellosa.com* for correlations to Common Core, state, national, and Canadian provincial standards.

Carson-Dellosa Publishing LLC
PO Box 35665
Greensboro, NC 27425 USA
carsondellosa.com

ISBN 978-1-4838-4160-1
01-002181151

Table of Contents

Introduction

Math 4 Today: Daily Skill Practice is a comprehensive yet quick and easy-to-use supplement to any classroom math curriculum. This series will strengthen students' math skills as they review numbers, operations, algebraic thinking, measurement, data, and geometry.

This book covers 40 weeks of daily practice. Essential math skills are reviewed each day during a four-day period with an assessment of the skills practiced on the fifth day. Each week includes a math fluency practice section, intended to be a quick one-minute activity that encourages fluency in math facts. For more detailed fluency tips, see pages 5 and 6. The week concludes with a math journal prompt.

Various skills and concepts are reinforced throughout the book through activities that align to the state standards. To view these standards, see the Standards Alignment Chart on page 7.

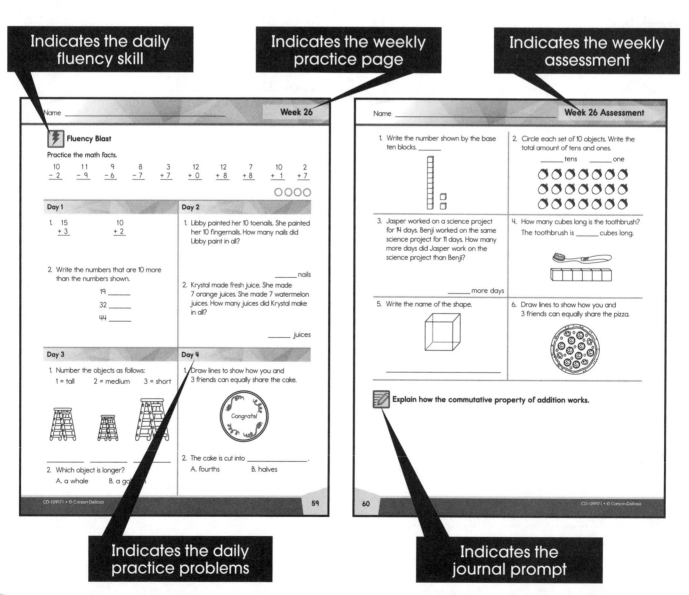

CD-104971 • © Carson-Dellosa

Developing Fluency

One of the primary goals of every teacher is to help students learn basic math facts accurately, recall them fluently, and retain that fluency over time. Fluency is the stage of learning where the learner acquires the information at an automatic level. A student must have this fluency of math facts in order to perform multi-digit algorithms and problem solve efficiently.

Math strategies should be introduced and reinforced daily to develop number sense. Opportunity is lost to develop number sense when math facts are taught only through rote memorization. The key to using strategies for basic facts is to have students discover the patterns in addition and multiplication and name them. For example, in addition, students may recognize doubles facts. In multiplication, students may see that 1 times any number equals the same number.

The ability to effortlessly recall math facts lessens students' anxiety and increases their confidence when engaging in more challenging math tasks.

Math Fluency Activities

Use these fun and easy games to engage students in practicing math facts.

- **Dice Roll**—Roll two dice. Use the numbers to practice adding, subtracting, multiplying, dividing, and creating fractions.
- **Flash Card Swat**—Using flash cards, students flip over two cards at a time. Students should use a flyswatter to swat a card they think they know the answer to and say the answer.
- **Race the Room**—Tape a long piece of bulletin board paper to a wall. Have teams of students stand on the opposite side of the room. Say math facts and have students race to the paper and write the answers.
- **War**—Using a deck of cards, students flip over two cards and add (or multiply). Whoever says the correct sum (or product) first keeps the cards.

Using the Fluency Blast

The fluency blast section is designed for students to use mental math on a daily basis. It is not intended that students write the answers each day. Students should practice the fluency blast facts for the week every day (excluding assessment day). Have students color a bubble for each day of practice. Begin the activity by setting a timer for one minute (or 30 seconds). To ensure students are practicing the math facts accurately, post an answer key on the first day.

Tracking Fluency

Have students use the reproducible on page 6 to track their progress. First, students should set a time for when they would like to meet their fluency goals. Then, they should fill in the blank spaces with the math facts they would like to practice. Finally, have students color a section as they master each goal. This page can be used monthly, quarterly, or throughout the entire school year.

Name _____

Fact Fluency Blastoff!

My goal is to know all of my _____ facts

by _____ .

Fact

Fact

Fact

Fact

Fact

Fact

Fact

Fact

Fact

Fact

I know
all of my
_____
facts!

Standards Alignment Chart

State Standards*		Weeks
Operations and Algebraic Thinking		
Represent and solve problems involving addition and subtraction.	1.OA.1, 1.OA.2	1–40
Understand and apply properties of operations and the relationship between addition and subtraction.	1.OA.3, 1.OA.4	1–40
Add and subtract within 20.	1.OA.5, 1.OA.6	1–40
Work with addition and subtraction equations.	1.OA.7, 1.OA.8	1–40
Number and Operations in Base Ten		
Extend the counting sequence.	1.NBT.1	1–5, 7–10, 14, 15
Understand place value.	1.NBT.2, 1.NBT.3	5, 12, 13, 16, 18–21, 23, 25–28, 30, 32, 34, 35, 39
Use place value understanding and properties of operations to add and subtract.	1.NBT.4–1.NBT.6	1–40
Measurement and Data		
Measure lengths indirectly and by iterating length units.	1.MD.1, 1.MD.2	16–29
Tell and write time.	1.MD.3	1–15, 28, 30–32, 35–40
Represent and interpret data.	1.MD.4	16, 17, 33, 34, 37, 38
Geometry		
Reason with shapes and their attributes.	1.G.1–1.G.3	1–40

The research is clear that family involvement is strongly linked to student success. Support for student learning at home improves student achievement in school. Educators should not underestimate the significance of this connection.

The fluency activities in this book create an opportunity to create or improve this school-to-home link. Students are encouraged to practice their math fluency facts at home with their families each week. Parents and guardians can use the reproducible tracking sheet (below) to record how their students performed in their fluency practice during the week. Students should be encouraged to return their tracking sheets to the teacher at the end of the week.

In order to make the school-to-home program work for students and their families, it may be helpful to reach out to them with an introductory letter. Explain the program and its intent and ask them to partner with you in their children's educational process. Describe the role you expect them to play. Encourage them to offer suggestions or feedback along the way.

Name _____ Week of _____

Fact Fluency: Practice Makes Perfect!

Day	Fact(s) I practiced	How I practiced	How I feel about these facts
M		☐ flash cards ☐ worksheet ☐ game ☐ other _____	☺ ☹
T		☐ flash cards ☐ worksheet ☐ game ☐ other _____	☺ ☹
W		☐ flash cards ☐ worksheet ☐ game ☐ other _____	☺ ☹
Th		☐ flash cards ☐ worksheet ☐ game ☐ other _____	☺ ☹

Fluency Blast

Practice the math facts.

10	10	8	5	8	5	7	9	6	9
− 3	− 8	− 6	− 5	− 0	− 2	− 7	− 6	− 3	− 4

○○○○

Day 1

1. Write the number that makes each number sentence true.

   _____ − 6 = 3

   _____ − 3 = 8

2. Write **true** or **false**. _____

   9 + 3 = 3 + 8

3. Draw base ten blocks to show the number 12.

Day 2

1. Kenny has 4 video games. Kenny buys 2 more video games. How many video games does Kenny have in all?

   _____ + _____ = _____ games

2. Mitch skated for 1 hour on Monday. On Wednesday, Mitch skated for 4 hours. How many hours did Mitch skate in all?

   _____ + _____ = _____ hours

Day 3

1. Draw hands on the clock to show 11:30.

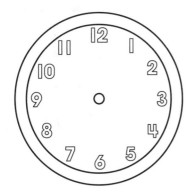

2. What time do you eat lunch at school?

   _____

Day 4

1. Circle the name of the shape.

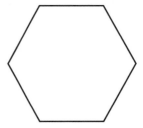

   A. hexagon   B. circle

2. How many sides does it have? _____

3. Color half of the shape red.

1. Draw base ten blocks to show the number 17.

2. If 8 + 8 + 2 = 18, then 8 + 2 + 8 = _____.

3. Dion has 9 bananas. He gives away 3 bananas. How many bananas does Dion have left?

_____ – _____ = _____ bananas

4. Draw hands on the clock to show 2:30.

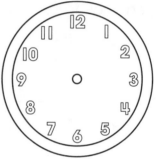

5. Draw a hexagon.

6. How many corners does a hexagon have? _____

 What are some ways you can measure an object?

Fluency Blast

Practice the math facts.

10	8	10	10	9	5	10	9	8	7
− 4	− 0	− 7	− 9	− 8	− 0	− 8	− 9	− 8	− 5

○○○○

Day 1

1. Count the objects to help you solve the problem.

   _____ − _____ = _____

2. Write the number word for each number.

   7 _____   10 _____

Day 2

1. Donny catches 5 fish in a pond. Donny catches 6 fish in a river. How many fish did Donny catch in all?

   _____ + _____ = _____ fish

2. Jay sells 3 cups of lemonade during the morning. In the afternoon, Jay sells 7 cups of lemonade. How many cups of lemonade does Jay sell in all?

   _____ + _____ = _____ cups

Day 3

1. Draw hands on the clock to show 7:30.

   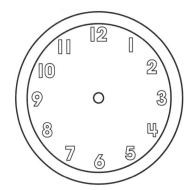

2. Circle the time when someone might eat dinner.

   A. 7:30 am   B. 7:30 pm

Day 4

1. Color the solid shapes.

2. Choose one solid shape. Describe it.

   _____

   _____

1. Draw a line to match each number word to its number.

   twenty-eight   14

   fourteen   5

   five   28

2. Write the number that makes the number sentence true.

   _____ − 5 = 8

3. Write **true** or **false**. _____

   9 − 3 = 8 − 2

4. Draw hands on the clock to show 8:30.

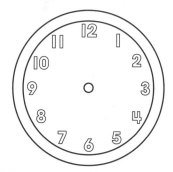

5. Use two square pattern blocks to make a rectangle. Trace the shape.

6. Draw an **X** on the flat shape.

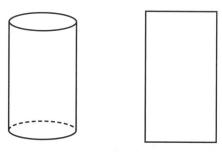

 Why is it important to be able to tell time?

Fluency Blast

Practice the math facts.

$$\begin{array}{ccccccccc} 10 & 7 & 8 & 10 & 9 & 10 & 7 & 9 & 10 & 9 \\ -7 & -6 & -6 & -5 & -0 & -2 & -7 & -1 & -10 & -8 \end{array}$$

○○○○

Day 1

1. Write **true** or **false**. _____

   $$12 - 7 = 11 - 6$$

2. Write the number that makes the number sentence true.

   $$18 - \text{_____} = 4$$

3. Draw a line to match each number word to its number.

sixteen	16
four	20
twenty	4

Day 2

1. There were 17 grapes. Maddie ate 4 grapes. How many grapes are left?

   _____ – _____ = _____ grapes

2. There were 12 carrots. Petunia the hamster ate 2 carrots. How many carrots are left?

   _____ – _____ = _____ carrots

Day 3

1. Show 6:30 on the clock.

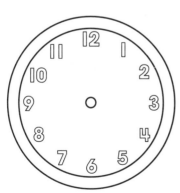

2. Circle the correct way to write the time in words.

   A. six three   B. half past six

Day 4

1. Use 3 triangles to make a trapezoid. Trace the shape.

2. How many corners does it have? _____

3. Describe the new shape. _____

   _____

1. Write the number that makes each number sentence true.

   17 − _____ = 1

   20 − _____ = 10

2.   7
     8
   + 3
   ‾‾‾

3. Nellie wrote 10 letters on Monday. She wrote 6 more letters on Tuesday. How many total letters did Nellie write on Monday and Tuesday?

   _____ + _____ = _____ letters

4. Draw hands on the clock to show 12:30.

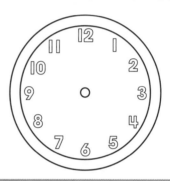

5. Color the trapezoids.

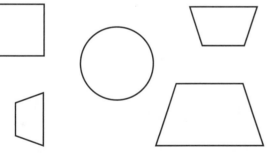

6. Draw a line to match each number word to its number.

   nineteen   5

   twelve   12

   five   19

 When we lose an object, do we subtract or add? Why?

Fluency Blast

Practice the math facts.

9	8	10	9	8	4	10	10	10	9
− 4	− 8	− 6	− 2	− 4	− 4	− 8	− 1	− 5	− 6

○○○○

Day 1

1. Write **true** or **false**. _____

   5 − 4 = 7 − 6

2. Write the number shown by the base ten blocks. _____

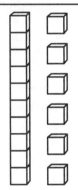

Day 2

1. Lamonte buys 12 gallons of punch for the party. He serves 9 gallons of punch during the party. How many gallons of punch does Lamonte have left?

   _____ − _____ = _____ gallons

2. Mom picked 12 flowers in the field. She picked 4 more flowers by the house. How many flowers did Mom pick in all?

   _____ + _____ = _____ flowers

Day 3

1. How many cubes long is the pencil?

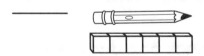

2. Ask 10 friends which playground activity is their favorite. Use tally marks to show their answers.

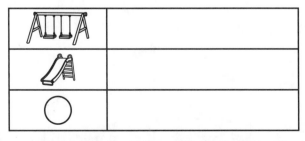

Day 4

1. Color the squares.

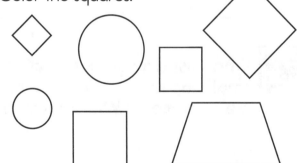

2. Name one defining attribute of a square.

   _____

   _____

1. Draw base ten blocks to show the number 17.

2.   8
     8
   + 4
   ___

3. Leo bought 15 pieces of gum. He chewed 10 pieces. How many pieces of gum does Leo have left?

   _____ – _____ = _____ pieces

4. How many paper clips long is the comb?

   The comb is _____ paper clips long.

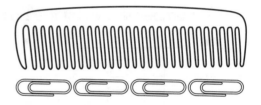

5. Divide the square into 4 equal parts.

   The square is divided into _____.

   A. fourths   B. halves

6. Draw a pattern with squares and trapezoids.

   Describe your pattern.

   _____

   _____

 Ethan used large paper clips to measure his pencil box. Jack used small paper clips to measure his pencil box. Did they get the same measurement? Why or why not?

Fluency Blast

Practice the math facts.

10	10	8	5	1	8	7	9	5	10
− 3	− 10	− 1	+ 0	− 0	− 3	− 7	− 6	− 5	− 1

○○○○

Day 1

1. Write the number that makes each number sentence true.

    _____ − 6 = 4

    _____ − 8 = 3

2. Write **true** or **false**. _____

    9 − 1 = 12 − 4

3. Use mental math to solve.

    30 − 10 = _____

    40 − 10 = _____

Day 2

1. Jimmy ran for 3 hours on Saturday. He ran for 4 more hours on Sunday. How many total hours did Jimmy run on Saturday and Sunday?

    _____ + _____ = _____ hours

2. There are 12 blue erasers. There are 4 yellow erasers. How many erasers are there in all?

    _____ + _____ = _____ erasers

Day 3

1. How many paper clips long is the screwdriver? _____

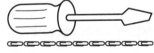

2. Ask 10 friends which drink they like best. Use tally marks to show their answers.

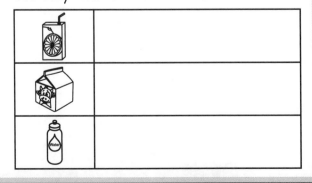

Day 4

1. Does this rectangle show equal parts? _____ Why or why not?

_____

2. Divide the rectangle into 4 equal parts.

1. Write **true** or **false**.

   _____

   12 − 5 = 10 − 3

2. 50 − 10 = _____

   40 − 20 = _____

   30 − 10 = _____

3. Sam picks 11 oranges. He picks 3 more oranges. How many oranges does Sam pick in all?

   _____ + _____ = _____ oranges

4. Number the objects as follows:

   1 = long   2 = medium   3 = short

   _____   _____   _____

5. Write the name of the shape.

   _____

6. How many corners does a rectangle have? _____

 Write an addition problem with three one-digit numbers. Have a friend solve it.

CD-104971 • © Carson-Dellosa

Name _____

 Fluency Blast

Practice the math facts.

7	9	8	9	4	8	10	9	6	9
− 4	− 9	− 8	− 5	− 4	− 0	− 8	− 9	− 5	− 8

○○○○

Day 1

1. Write **true** or **false**. _____

   9 − 7 = 8 − 6

2. 40 − 20 = _____

3. What is the value of the number?

   11

   _____ ten

   _____ ones

Day 2

1. Ben sees 7 rocks in the pond. He sees 9 more rocks. How many rocks does Ben see in the pond in all?

   _____ + _____ = _____ rocks

2. Porchia walked 8 miles with her mom on Saturday. Then, she walked 4 miles with her dad on Sunday. How many miles did Porchia walk in all?

   _____ + _____ = _____ miles

Day 3

1. Number the objects as follows:

   1 = long   2 = medium   3 = short

   _____ _____ _____

2. Circle the object that is longer.

   A. a shoelace   B. a finger

Day 4

1. Color the faces on the cylinder.

2. How many faces are there? _____

3. What real-world object is in the shape of a cylinder?

   A. can   B. box

1. Ryan saw 10 bees in a beehive. He saw 6 more bees go into the beehive. How many bees are in the beehive now?

   _____ + _____ = _____ bees

2. Write **true** or **false**.

   _____

   $13 - 4 = 9 - 5$

3. What is the value of the number?

   15

   _____ ten

   _____ ones

4. Number the objects as follows:

   1 = long   2 = medium   3 = short

    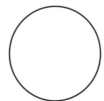

   _____   _____   _____

5. Write the name of the shape.

   _____

6. Draw an **X** on the flat shape.

   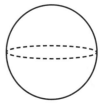

 Explain why a cylinder rolls but a cube does not.

Fluency Blast

Practice the math facts.

$$\begin{array}{cccccccccc} 10 & 7 & 8 & 10 & 8 & 9 & 10 & 9 & 7 & 9 \\ -3 & -5 & -6 & -0 & -0 & -0 & -1 & -6 & -6 & -8 \end{array}$$

○○○○

Day 1

1. Write the number that makes the number sentence true.

   _____ + 5 = 19

2. 20 − 8 = 12 + _____

3. What is the value of the number?

   19

   _____ ten

   _____ ones

Day 2

1. At night, 15 squirrels are in a tree. Later, 9 squirrels run away. How many squirrels are left in the tree?

   _____ − _____ = _____ squirrels

2. Maricela picked 15 carrots. She gave 3 to her neighbor. How many carrots does Maricela have left?

   _____ − _____ = _____ carrots

Day 3

1. Number the objects as follows:

   1 = long   2 = medium   3 = short

   _____ _____ _____

2. Circle the object that is shorter.

   A. a shovel   B. a toothbrush

Day 4

1. Match each shape to its name.

   cone   cube   cylinder

2. Which shape in question 1 has one face?

   _____

3. Write the number of sides and corners.

   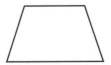

   _____ sides

   _____ corners

1. Write the number that makes the number sentence true.

    _____ + 1 = 18

2. Draw lines to show how you and 3 friends can equally share this graham cracker.

   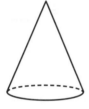

3. What is the value of the number?

    13

    _____ ten

    _____ ones

4. How many fish long is the fishing rod?

    The fishing rod is _____ fish long.

    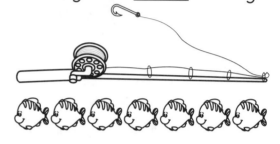

5. Write the name of the shape.

    _____

6. Draw a picture of a real-world object that is in the shape of a cone.

 If a family is adopting a new dog, are they adding to or subtracting from the family? Why?

Name _____

 Fluency Blast

Practice the math facts.

10	9	9	10	8	19	10	9	8	6
− 7	− 9	− 7	− 9	− 1	− 1	− 8	− 3	− 2	− 4

○○○○

Day 1

1. 15   6
   + 3   + 5

2. What is the value of the number?

   16

   _____ ten
   _____ ones

3. 20   30
   + 10   + 6

Day 2

1. We saw 16 narwhals playing in the water. We saw 3 swim away. How many narwhals are left playing in the water?

   _____ narwhals

2. There are 17 students playing on the playground. Three of the students leave to play in the sandbox. How many students are left playing on the playground?

   _____ students

Day 3

1. How many cubes long is the spoon?

   The spoon is _____ cubes long.

   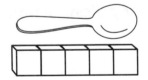

2. Circle the object that is taller.

   A. a giraffe   B. a cat

Day 4

1. Color the cubes.

   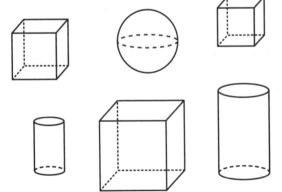

2. Name one defining attribute of a cube.

   _____
   _____

1.   60
    +10
    _____

2. Draw base ten blocks to show the number 16.

3. Write the number that makes the number sentence true.

   12 − _____ = 7

4. Number the objects as follows:

   1 = long   2 = medium   3 = short

   _____   _____   _____

5. Write the name of the shape.

   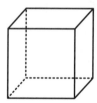

   _____

6. How many faces does a cube have?

   _____

 What shapes do you see when you walk in your neighborhood?

Fluency Blast

Practice the math facts.

| $\begin{array}{r}8\\-3\end{array}$ | $\begin{array}{r}10\\-6\end{array}$ | $\begin{array}{r}9\\-1\end{array}$ | $\begin{array}{r}7\\-5\end{array}$ | $\begin{array}{r}8\\+2\end{array}$ | $\begin{array}{r}4\\+0\end{array}$ | $\begin{array}{r}7\\+2\end{array}$ | $\begin{array}{r}3\\+10\end{array}$ | $\begin{array}{r}10\\-10\end{array}$ | $\begin{array}{r}8\\-4\end{array}$ |

○○○○

Day 1

1. $12 - 9 = 2 +$ _____

2. Write the number that makes the number sentence true.

    $15 -$ _____ $= 12$

3. What is the value of the number?

    10

    _____ ten

    _____ ones

Day 2

1. There are 17 children playing in the pool. Some children leave for the day. Now, there are 14 children in the pool. How many children left for the day?

    _____ children

2. Dad bought Jill a new box of markers. There were 10 markers in the box. When Jill opened the box, 4 markers fell on the ground. How many markers are left in the box?

    _____ markers

Day 3

1. Number the objects as follows:

    1 = long   2 = medium   3 = short

    _____   _____   _____

2. Circle the object that is longer.

    A. a water hose   B. a football field

Day 4

1. Circle the set of shapes that form this figure when put together.

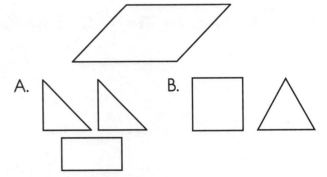

    A.   B.

2. How many corners does the figure have? _____

3. How many sides does it have? _____

---

1. Write the number that makes the number sentence true.

   21 − _____ = 10

2.   9   11
    − 6   − 3

3. What is the value of the number?

   17

   _____ ten

   _____ ones

4. Number the objects as follows:

   1 = long   2 = medium   3 = short

   _____   _____   _____

5. Circle the set of shapes that form this figure when put together.

   A.   B.

6. How many sides does a circle have?

   _____

 Will says 2 + 10 = 12. Uri says 10 + 2 = 12. Who is right? Explain.

Fluency Blast

Practice the math facts.

10	9	10	10	4	10	9	8	6	6
− 4	− 1	− 5	− 9	+ 10	− 8	+ 3	− 2	+ 4	− 4

○○○○

Day 1

1. 15   16
    + 3   + 4

2. 50   40
    −40   − 10

Day 2

1. Clarissa ate 1 apple for breakfast. She ate 17 strawberries for a snack. How many pieces of fruit did Clarissa eat in all?

_____ pieces of fruit

2. Mario gave 11 cupcakes to the boys in his classroom. He gave 9 cupcakes to the girls. How many cupcakes did Mario give out in all?

_____ cupcakes

Day 3

1. Number the objects as follows:

    1 = long   2 = medium   3 = short

_____ _____ _____

2. Circle the object that is shorter.

   A. a chair   B. a door

Day 4

1. Draw one side to complete the shape. Circle the name of the shape.

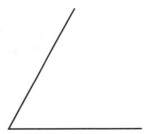

square   triangle   rectangle

2. How many corners does it have? _____

3. Color half of the shape green.

---

1. 50 – 30 = _____

   70 – 20 = _____

2. Write the number that makes the number sentence true.

   _____ + 4 = 24

3. Javier ate 11 mints yesterday. He ate 7 mints today. How many mints did Javier eat in all?

   _____ mints

4. How many fish tall is the fisherman?

   The fisherman is _____ fish tall.

5. Write the name of the shape.

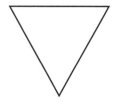

   _____

6. Draw a picture of a real-world object that is in the shape of a triangle.

 What objects can you draw with triangles? Draw a picture and use at least 3 triangles in your drawing. Label the objects.

CD-104971 • © Carson-Dellosa

Fluency Blast

Practice the math facts.

$$\begin{array}{cc} 7 \\ -3 \end{array} \quad \begin{array}{cc} 10 \\ -7 \end{array} \quad \begin{array}{cc} 10 \\ -6 \end{array} \quad \begin{array}{cc} 9 \\ -5 \end{array} \quad \begin{array}{cc} 8 \\ +3 \end{array} \quad \begin{array}{cc} 4 \\ +4 \end{array} \quad \begin{array}{cc} 0 \\ +0 \end{array} \quad \begin{array}{cc} 9 \\ +1 \end{array} \quad \begin{array}{cc} 10 \\ -6 \end{array} \quad \begin{array}{cc} 9 \\ -7 \end{array}$$

○○○○

Day 1

1. Write the number that makes the number sentence true.

_____ + 7 = 11

2. Write the number shown by the base ten blocks. _____

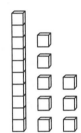

3. 12 − 3 = 3 + _____

Day 2

1. Tisha counted 20 roses on a rosebush. She picked 3 roses. How many roses are left on the rosebush?

_____ roses

2. I watched 20 dolphins race in the water. I saw 6 dolphins stop to watch fish. How many dolphins are still racing?

_____ dolphins

Day 3

1. How many fish long is the boat?

The boat is _____ fish long.

2. Circle the object that is taller.

A. a bike   B. a truck

Day 4

1. Draw one side to complete the shape. Circle the name of the shape.

trapezoid   triangle   rectangle

2. What real-world object is in the shape of a rectangle?

A. a soccer field   B. a shoe

1.
$$\begin{array}{r} 8 \\ +\ 6 \\ \hline \end{array}$$
$$\begin{array}{r} 4 \\ -\ 2 \\ \hline \end{array}$$

$$\begin{array}{r} 6 \\ +\ 6 \\ \hline \end{array}$$
$$\begin{array}{r} 9 \\ -\ 6 \\ \hline \end{array}$$

2. Write the numbers that make the number sentences true.

_____ + 3 = 14

_____ + 5 = 9

_____ + 0 = 10

3. Yuri's aunt gave her 13 pictures to decorate her notebook. Yuri gave 9 pictures to her best friend. How many pictures does Yuri have left?

_____ pictures

4. Number the objects as follows:

1 = long   2 = medium   3 = short

_____ _____ _____

5. Write the name of the shape.

_____

6. Draw a picture of a real-world object that is in the shape of a rectangle.

 Lydia solved this problem: 20 + 10 = 10. Is she correct? What did she do wrong? Explain.

Fluency Blast

Practice the math facts.

| $\begin{array}{r} 10 \\ -\ 4 \\ \hline \end{array}$ | $\begin{array}{r} 10 \\ -\ 8 \\ \hline \end{array}$ | $\begin{array}{r} 8 \\ -\ 3 \\ \hline \end{array}$ | $\begin{array}{r} 10 \\ -\ 9 \\ \hline \end{array}$ | $\begin{array}{r} 10 \\ +\ 7 \\ \hline \end{array}$ | $\begin{array}{r} 9 \\ +\ 0 \\ \hline \end{array}$ | $\begin{array}{r} 2 \\ +\ 10 \\ \hline \end{array}$ | $\begin{array}{r} 6 \\ +\ 2 \\ \hline \end{array}$ | $\begin{array}{r} 10 \\ -\ 5 \\ \hline \end{array}$ | $\begin{array}{r} 10 \\ -\ 2 \\ \hline \end{array}$ |

○○○○

Day 1

1. $15 + 4 =$ _____

   $10 + 9 =$ _____

2. $\begin{array}{r} 47 \\ +\ 2 \\ \hline \end{array}$ $\qquad$ $\begin{array}{r} 36 \\ +\ 4 \\ \hline \end{array}$

3. Write the number that makes the number sentence true.

   _____ $+ 10 = 18$

Day 2

1. Farmer Edgar planted 14 watermelon seeds. Birds ate 4 seeds. How many watermelon seeds are left?

   _____ watermelon seeds

2. Byron has 10 baseball bats. He gives away 4 bats. How many baseball bats are left?

   _____ baseball bats

Day 3

1. Number the objects as follows:

   1 = long   2 = medium   3 = short

   _____ _____ _____

2. Circle the object that is longer.

   A. a mouse   B. a bee

Day 4

1. Draw one side to complete the shape. Circle the name of the shape.

   square   triangle   rectangle

2. How many sides does it have? _____

3. Draw lines to divide the shape into fourths.

---

1. 12   22
    + 4   + 2

2. Write **true** or **false**.

    _____

    $5 + 9 = 7 + 7$

3. Write the number that makes the number sentence true.

    $30 - \underline{\hspace{1cm}} = 7$

4. Number the objects as follows:

    1 = long   2 = medium   3 = short

    _____ _____ _____

5. Color the squares.

6. Draw a picture of a real-world object that is in the shape of a square.

 How do you measure your height? Explain.

Fluency Blast

Practice the math facts.

$$\begin{array}{c} 10 \\ -\ 6 \end{array} \qquad \begin{array}{c} 10 \\ -\ 3 \end{array} \qquad \begin{array}{c} 8 \\ -\ 0 \end{array} \qquad \begin{array}{c} 7 \\ -\ 5 \end{array} \qquad \begin{array}{c} 8 \\ -\ 7 \end{array} \qquad \begin{array}{c} 4 \\ +\ 6 \end{array} \qquad \begin{array}{c} 7 \\ +\ 10 \end{array} \qquad \begin{array}{c} 10 \\ -\ 0 \end{array} \qquad \begin{array}{c} 10 \\ +\ 7 \end{array} \qquad \begin{array}{c} 10 \\ -\ 7 \end{array}$$

○○○○

Day 1

1. Draw base ten blocks to show the number 14.

2. Write the number that makes the number sentence true.

$$18 - \underline{\qquad} = 13$$

3. Write the number that is 10 more than the number shown.

49 _____

Day 2

1. Adrienne hiked for 7 hours. She hiked for 5 more hours the next day. How many hours did Adrienne hike in all?

_____ hours

2. Charlotte has 11 aunts on her mom's side. She has 7 aunts on her dad's side. How many aunts does Charlotte have in all?

_____ aunts

Day 3

1. Number the objects as follows:

1 = long   2 = medium   3 = short

_____ _____ _____

2. Circle the object that is taller.

A. a house   B. a flower

Day 4

1. Draw a line to show how you and 1 friend can equally share the apple pie.

1. Draw base ten blocks to show 18.

2. Write the numbers that make the number sentences true.

   15 − _____ = 8

   22 − _____ = 10

3. Write the numbers that are 10 more than the numbers shown.

   28 _____

   68 _____

4. Number the objects as follows:

   1 = long   2 = medium   3 = short

   _____ _____ _____

5. Name one defining attribute of a circle.

   _____

   _____

   _____

   _____

6. Draw a line to show how you and 1 friend can equally share the cookie.

 Explain how to use a number line.

CD-104971 • © Carson-Dellosa

Fluency Blast

Practice the math facts.

10	11	9	8	3	12	12	7	10	2
− 2	− 9	− 6	− 7	+ 7	+ 0	+ 8	+ 8	+ 1	+ 7

○○○○

Day 1

1.
```
  15        10
+  3      +  2
```

2. Write the numbers that are 10 more than the numbers shown.

   19 _____

   32 _____

   44 _____

Day 2

1. Libby painted her 10 toenails. She painted her 10 fingernails. How many nails did Libby paint in all?

   _____ nails

2. Krystal made fresh juice. She made 7 orange juices. She made 7 watermelon juices. How many juices did Krystal make in all?

   _____ juices

Day 3

1. Number the objects as follows:

   1 = tall   2 = medium   3 = short

   _____ _____ _____

2. Circle the object that is longer.

   A. a whale   B. a goldfish

Day 4

1. Draw lines to show how you and 3 friends can equally share the cake.

   Congrats!

2. The cake is cut into _____.

   A. fourths   B. halves

---

1. Write the number shown by the base ten blocks. _____

2. Circle each set of 10 objects. Write the total amount of tens and ones.

_____ tens   _____ one

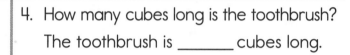

3. Jasper worked on a science project for 14 days. Benji worked on the same science project for 11 days. How many more days did Jasper work on the science project than Benji?

_____ more days

4. How many cubes long is the toothbrush?

The toothbrush is _____ cubes long.

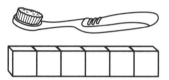

5. Write the name of the shape.

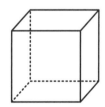

_____

6. Draw lines to show how you and 3 friends can equally share the pizza.

 Explain how the commutative property of addition works.

Fluency Blast

Practice the math facts.

10	2	8	5	10	9	10	8	10	10
− 2	+ 5	− 7	− 5	+ 0	− 2	+ 3	+ 3	+ 9	+ 5

○○○○

Day 1

1. Write <, >, or =.

   40 ◯ 37

2. Write the number that is 10 less than the number shown.

   _____ 16

3. Write the number that is 10 more than the number shown.

   86 _____

Day 2

1. Ashton orders 8 wraps. There are 5 ham wraps. How many wraps are not ham?

   _____ wraps

2. Pedro jumped over 13 small rocks. Then, he jumped over 4 more rocks. How many rocks did Pedro jump over in all?

   _____ rocks

Day 3

1. How many cubes long is the fork?

   The fork is _____ cubes long.

2. Circle the object that is longer.

   A. a spoon   B. a table

Day 4

1. Divide the rectangle into 2 equal parts.

2. The rectangle is divided into _____.

   A. fourths   B. halves

Name _____

1. Write <, >, or =.

   35 ◯ 35

   51 ◯ 15

2. Write the number that is 10 more than the number shown.

   26 _____

   Write the number that is 10 less than the number shown.

   _____ 83

3. Circle each set of 10 objects. Write the total amount of tens and ones.

   _____ ten   _____ ones

4. How many tennis balls long is the tennis racket?

   The tennis racket is _____ tennis balls long.

5. Divide the square in half. Color half of the square blue.

6. Draw something that is longer than an ant.

 Write a subtraction problem. Use drawings to show how you must "take away" objects to get to the answer. Solve the problem.

Fluency Blast

Practice the math facts.

| $\begin{array}{r}9\\-4\end{array}$ | $\begin{array}{r}10\\-9\end{array}$ | $\begin{array}{r}10\\-6\end{array}$ | $\begin{array}{r}10\\-10\end{array}$ | $\begin{array}{r}4\\+9\end{array}$ | $\begin{array}{r}4\\+5\end{array}$ | $\begin{array}{r}2\\+4\end{array}$ | $\begin{array}{r}9\\+1\end{array}$ | $\begin{array}{r}10\\+6\end{array}$ | $\begin{array}{r}10\\+1\end{array}$ |

○○○○

Day 1

1. Circle each set of 10 objects. Write the total amount of tens and ones.

   _____ tens   _____ ones

2. Write <, >, or =.

   22 ◯ 44

3. 70 − 10 = _____

Day 2

1. Kara stamped 9 packages. She stamped 7 more packages later. How many packages did Kara stamp in all?

   _____ packages

2. Aunt Joyce had 24 sunflowers in her garden. An animal ate 1 sunflower. How many sunflowers are left?

   _____ sunflowers

Day 3

1. How many buttons tall is the notebook?

   The notebook is _____ buttons tall.

2. Circle the object that is shorter.

   A. a skateboard   B. a golf club

Day 4

1. Divide the rectangle into 4 equal parts.

2. The rectangle is divided into _____ .

   A. halves   B. fourths

1. Circle each set of 10 objects. Write the total amount of tens and ones.

_____ ten   _____ ones

2. Write <, >, or =.

14 ◯ 32

21 ◯ 12

3.   19   15
    + 6   + 5

4. Write the time shown on the clock.

_____

5. Divide the circle into 4 equal parts.

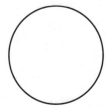

The circle is divided into _____.

A. halves   B. fourths

6. If you divide a circle in half, how many equal parts are there? _____

 Your friend gives you a candy bar. You have to share it with 3 people. How many pieces do you need so that you can have a piece too? Draw a picture to explain.

CD-104971 • © Carson-Dellosa

Fluency Blast

Practice the math facts.

10	7	9	10	8	4	7	2	8	10
− 3	− 5	− 5	− 5	+ 9	+ 3	+ 2	+ 6	+ 2	− 1

○○○○

Day 1

1. Write <, >, or =.

    75 ◯ 95

    59 ◯ 39

2. Write the number that is 10 less than the number shown.

    _____ 52

3. What number comes before 99?

    _____

Day 2

1. Brayden sells 12 magazines in one day. He sells 6 magazines the next day. How many more magazines did Brayden sell on the first day?

    _____ more magazines

2. Simone received 18 text messages last Wednesday. She received only 5 text messages last Thursday. How many more texts did Simone receive on Wednesday?

    _____ text messages

Day 3

1. How many nails long is the hammer?

    The hammer is _____ nails long.

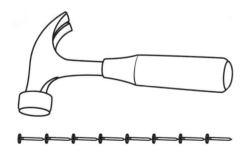

2. Circle the object that is longer.

    A. a bus   B. a train

Day 4

1. Color the trapezoids.

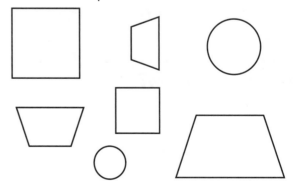

2. What shapes can you find in a trapezoid?

    A. triangles   B. circles

1. Write <, >, or =.

    52 $\bigcirc$ 21

    17 $\bigcirc$ 19

2. Write the number that is 10 more than the number shown.

    61 _____

    Write the number that is 10 less than the number shown.

    _____ 15

3. Gerardo's yard has 11 trees. Only 5 trees have leaves. The rest do not. How many of the trees do not have leaves?

    _____ trees

4. How many hands tall is the horse?

    The horse is _____ hands tall.

5. Write the name of the shape.

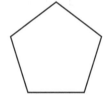

    _____

6. Draw a picture using trapezoids, rectangles, and circles.

 If you share one-half of your mac and cheese, how much is left? How do you know?

Fluency Blast

Practice the math facts.

| $\begin{array}{r} 10 \\ -4 \\ \hline \end{array}$ | $\begin{array}{r} 10 \\ -9 \\ \hline \end{array}$ | $\begin{array}{r} 10 \\ -6 \\ \hline \end{array}$ | $\begin{array}{r} 9 \\ -1 \\ \hline \end{array}$ | $\begin{array}{r} 10 \\ +7 \\ \hline \end{array}$ | $\begin{array}{r} 9 \\ +0 \\ \hline \end{array}$ | $\begin{array}{r} 10 \\ +8 \\ \hline \end{array}$ | $\begin{array}{r} 10 \\ +6 \\ \hline \end{array}$ | $\begin{array}{r} 8 \\ -1 \\ \hline \end{array}$ | $\begin{array}{r} 7 \\ -2 \\ \hline \end{array}$ |

○○○○

Day 1

1. $\begin{array}{r} 61 \\ +8 \\ \hline \end{array}$ $\begin{array}{r} 40 \\ +7 \\ \hline \end{array}$

2. What is the value of the number?

    30

    _____ tens

    _____ ones

3. Write the number that is 10 more than the number shown.

    55 _____

Day 2

1. Janelle picks 14 flowers in a field. She picks 3 more flowers at her house. How many flowers does Janelle pick in all?

    _____ flowers

2. Josh taught his new puppy some tricks. He taught him 6 tricks on Wednesday and 7 tricks on Thursday. How many tricks did Josh teach his puppy?

    _____ tricks

Day 3

1. Write the time shown on the clock.

    _____

2. Circle the correct way to write the time in words.

    A. 9 o six   B. nine thirty

Day 4

1. Color the triangles.

    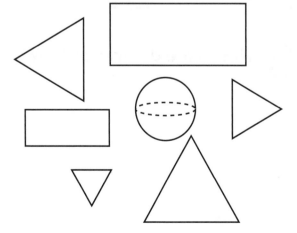

2. Name one attribute of a triangle.

    _____

1. What is the value of the number?

    60

    _____ tens

    _____ ones

2. Write the number that is 10 more than the number shown.

    82 _____

    Write the number that is 10 less than the number shown.

    _____ 82

3. Out of a class of 18 students, 7 students have straight hair. How many students do not have straight hair?

    _____ students

4. Write the time shown on the clock.

    _____

5. Write the name of the shape.

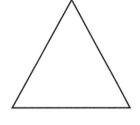

    _____

6. Draw a picture using triangles and rectangles.

 What is the difference between time on a clock and a timer on a stove?

Fluency Blast

Practice the math facts.

1	10	8	10	18	5	10	9	19	11
+ 3	− 4	+ 7	− 3	+ 1	− 2	+ 2	− 6	+ 0	+ 1

○○○○

Day 1

1. Write <, >, or =.

   56 ◯ 26

2. Write the number that is 10 less than the number shown.

   _____ 39

3. 13 + 12 = _____

Day 2

1. Spencer has 5 sports DVDs. He has 2 action DVDs. How many DVDs does Spencer have in all?

   _____ DVDs

2. Yasmin inflates 17 purple balloons. She inflates 3 green balloons. How many balloons does Yasmin inflate in all?

   _____ balloons

Day 3

1. Write the time shown on the clock.

   _____

2. Circle the correct way to write the time in words.

   A. seven thirty   B. 7-six

Day 4

1. Circle the name of the shape.

   A. square   B. half circle

2. How many sides does it have? _____

3. Color half of the shape red.

1. Write the number that is 10 more than the number shown.

    23 _____

    Write the number that is 10 less than the number shown.

    _____ 88

2. Write <, >, or =.

    61 ◯ 31

    22 ◯ 50

3. Patsy scores 2 goals on Saturday. She scores 5 goals on Sunday. How many more goals does Patsy score on Sunday?

     _____ more goals

4. Write the time shown on the clock.

    _____

5. Write the name of the shape.

    _____

6. Circle the real-world object that has the same shape as a half circle.

    A.    B.

 Can you count by tens starting at 7? If so, which numbers would you say?

Fluency Blast

Practice the math facts.

13	10	15	13	4	4	12	9	11	19
+ 1	− 9	+ 1	− 0	+ 10	− 0	+ 0	− 9	+ 1	+ 0

○○○○

Day 1

1. 44   73
    + 6   + 6

2. What is the value of the number?

    80

    _____ tens

    _____ ones

3. 50 − 10 = _____

    50 − 20 = _____

Day 2

1. Ellen bought 12 cookies at the store. But, 8 cookies broke on the way home. How many unbroken cookies does Ellen have left?

    _____ cookies

2. Mario sold 19 boxes of apples on Monday. He sold 7 boxes of apples on Friday. How many more boxes of apples did Mario sell on Monday?

    _____ more boxes

Day 3

1. Write the time shown on the clock.

    _____

2. Circle the correct way to write the time in words.

    A. two o'clock   B. 2 oclock

Day 4

1. Circle the rhombus.

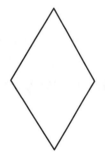 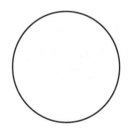

2. How many sides does it have? _____

3. Color half of the rhombus orange.

---

1. What is the value of the number?

   40

   _____ tens

   _____ ones

2. Write the number that is 10 less than the number shown.

   _____ 65

   Write the number that is 10 more than the number shown.

   29 _____

3. Write <, >, or =.

   27 ◯ 38

   46 ◯ 46

4. Write the time shown on the clock.

   _____

5. Color the rhombus.

   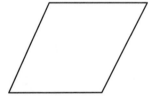 

6. If you divide a shape into fourths, how many equal parts are there?

   _____

 There were 3 books on the table. Ana left 2 more books on the table. How many books were on the table? Jamie says the answer is 1 book. Is Jamie right? Why or why not?

CD-104971 • © Carson-Dellosa

Fluency Blast

Practice the math facts.

19	10	8	5	8	11	7	10	10	6
+ 1	− 5	+ 8	− 5	+ 0	− 1	+ 7	− 6	+ 10	+ 5

○○○○

Day 1

1. 52 + 20 = _____

2. Write <, >, or =.

   28 ◯ 8

3. Write the number that is 10 more than the number shown.

   41

Day 2

1. Jenny practices soccer for 3 hours on Tuesday. She practices soccer for 4 hours on Wednesday. How many hours did Jenny practice soccer in all?

   _____hours

2. Allan has 12 peaches. Jake has 9 peaches. How many peaches do Allan and Jake have altogether?

   _____peaches

Day 3

1. Look at the tally chart. How many more blue cars were on the road than red cars?

Cars on the Road		
Blue	Red	White
||||	||	|||

   _____more blue cars were on the road than red cars.

Day 4

1. Circle the triangle.

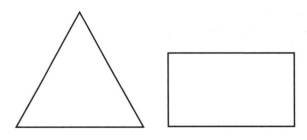

2. How many sides does it have? _____
3. Color half of the triangle yellow.

1. 18 + 70 = _____

   30 + 14 = _____

2. What is the value of the number?

   90

   _____ tens

   _____ ones

3. Ursula has 20 baseball posters in her room. She gives away 11 posters. How many posters does Ursula have left?

   _____ posters

4. Look at the tally chart. How many more snowy days were there in January than in March?

Snowy Days		
January	February	March
卌 卌 lll	卌 卌	卌 lll

   There were _____ more snowy days.

5. Draw a new shape with 3 triangles.

6. How many sides does the new shape in question 5 have? _____

 Write an addition or subtraction word problem about being at a beach.

Fluency Blast

Practice the math facts.

15	1	11	5	14	4	17	9	20	10
− 1	+ 12	− 2	+ 1	− 4	+ 9	− 1	+ 10	− 10	− 9

○○○○

Day 1

1. What is the value of the number?

   50

   _____ ones

   _____ tens

2. 63   27
   + 12   + 31

3. 90 − 30 = _____

   70 − 40 = _____

Day 2

1. Brian has 10 more toy cars than Paul has. Paul has 25 toy cars. How many toy cars does Brian have?

   _____ toy cars

2. There are 19 peaches in a basket. Only 9 peaches are ripe. How many peaches are not ripe?

   _____ peaches

Day 3

1. Look at the tally chart. How many more people like purple than orange?

Favorite Colors		
Orange	Purple	Yellow
III	₩₩ II	₩₩ I

_____ more people like purple.

Day 4

1. Draw two different ways to divide the rectangles in half.

2. The rectangles are divided into _____.

   A. fourths   B. halves

---

1. Look at the tally chart. What color of hair do most people have?

Hair Color		
Brown	Black	Blonde
ⅢⅢ Ⅲ	ⅢⅢ Ⅰ	Ⅲ

Most people have _____ hair.

2. 25 + 70 = _____

   31 + 40 = _____

3. Shane hangs 10 pictures one day. He hangs 8 pictures the next day. How many pictures does Shane hang in all?

   _____ pictures

4. Write the value of the number 73.

   _____ tens

   _____ ones

5. Draw a picture with squares, circles, and triangles.

6. Divide the circle into 4 equal parts. Color one part blue.

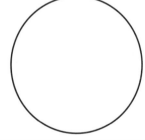

 Write an addition or subtraction word problem about being at a playground.

Fluency Blast

Practice the math facts.

3	10	7	10	9	14	9	9	4	10
+ 3	− 8	+ 7	− 5	+ 9	− 4	+ 2	− 7	+ 4	+ 10

○ ○ ○ ○

Day 1

1. What is the value of the number?

35

_____ tens

_____ ones

2. Write <, >, or =.

73 ◯ 53

3. Write the number that is 10 more than the number shown.

63 _____

Day 2

1. There is a basket with 12 marbles. Olivia takes 10 marbles out of the basket. How many marbles are in the basket now?

_____ marbles

2. Brian has 3 fewer chips than Ty. Ty has 7 chips. How many chips does Brian have?

_____ chips

Day 3

1. Write the time shown on the clock.

_____

2. What do you do at this time of the day?

_____

Day 4

1. Color the cones.

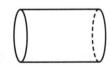

2. Circle the real-world shape that looks like a cone.

A.   B.

Name _____

Week 35 Assessment

1. Write the number that is 10 more than the number shown.

   43 _____

   Write the number that is 10 less than the number shown.

   _____ 64

2. What is the value of the number?

   11

   _____ ten
   _____ one

3. Khalil collected 13 lightning bugs in one jar. He collected 5 lightning bugs in another jar. How many lightning bugs did Khalil collect in all?

   _____ lightning bugs

4. Write the time shown on the clock.

   _____

5. Circle the objects that look like spheres.

6. Describe a sphere.

   _____
   _____
   _____
   _____

 Draw an analog clock. Label the parts.

78

CD-104971 • © Carson-Dellosa

Fluency Blast

Practice the math facts.

10	1	16	20	14	2	16	9	19	12
− 4	+ 9	− 6	− 0	− 7	+ 8	− 8	+ 0	− 8	− 6

○○○○

Day 1

1. Write <, >, or =.

    89 ◯ 89

2. Write the number that makes the number sentence true.

    11 + _____ = 16

3.   51   36
     + 8   + 13

Day 2

1. Jeff read 12 books. His friend Nathan read 5 books. How many more books did Jeff read?

    _____ more books

2. In a basketball game, Malik scored 12 points. James scored 16 points. How many points did Malik and James score altogether?

    _____ points

Day 3

1. Write the time shown on the clock.

    _____

2. What time do you go to bed? _____
    Is this **am** or **pm**? _____

Day 4

1. Color the half circles.

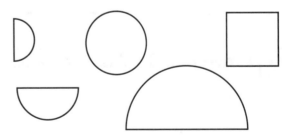

2. Draw a picture of a real-world object that is in the shape of a half circle.

1. Write <, >, or =.

    71 ◯ 24

    33 ◯ 53

2. Mackenzie drew 16 squares. She colored 5 squares orange. She left the rest of the squares white. How many squares did Mackenzie leave white?

    _____ squares

3. Kris bought 19 oak trees. She planted 8 oak trees in her front yard. How many oak trees does Kris have left to plant in her backyard?

    _____ oak trees

4. Write the time shown on the clock.

    _____

5. Draw a half circle.

6. Circle the defining attribute of the shape in question 5.

    A. It is shaped like a bowl.

    B. It has one side.

 Prove that 3 + 7 has the same sum as 6 + 4.

CD-104971 • © Carson-Dellosa

Fluency Blast

Practice the math facts.

13	15	12	10	20	13	9	10	18	16
− 3	+ 2	− 6	+ 5	− 0	+ 4	− 7	+ 6	− 9	− 8

○○○○ ○

Day 1

1. If 11 − 3 = 8, then 11 − 8 = _____.

2. Write the number that makes the number sentence true.

   15 + _____ = 25

3.
   ```
     89          28
   + 3         + 7
   ```

Day 2

1. There are 16 pairs of glasses. If 12 pairs of glasses are broken, how many pairs are not broken?

   _____ pairs

2. Greg had 20 shirts. He donated 8 shirts. How many shirts did Greg have left?

   _____ shirts

Day 3

Look at the tally chart. Use it to answer the questions.

Favorite Sports		
Soccer	Baseball	Football
IIII	II	III

1. Which sport do students like the most?
   _____

2. Which sport do students like the least?
   _____

Day 4

1. Color the rectangles. Circle the squares.

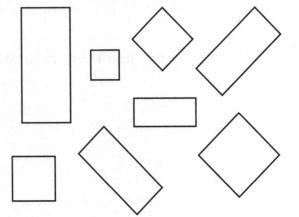

2. How many corners does each shape have? _____

1. Look at the tally chart. Who has the most pennies in her bank?

Pennies in the Piggy Bank		
Alexa	Grace	Lynn
卌 卌 卌	卌 卌	卌 |||| 卌 卌

_____ has the most pennies.

2. Write the number that makes the number sentence true.

$$\_\_\_\_\_ - 2 = 14$$

3. Judd has 17 stamps in his folder. He gives 7 stamps to his teacher. How many stamps does Judd have left in his folder?

_____ stamps

4. Write the time shown on the clock.

_____

5. Draw a square. Divide it into fourths.

6. Draw a picture with squares and rectangles.

 How long do you think it takes to bake a cake? Why?

Fluency Blast

Practice the math facts.

| $\begin{array}{r} 11 \\ +\ 2 \\ \hline \end{array}$ | $\begin{array}{r} 10 \\ -\ 9 \\ \hline \end{array}$ | $\begin{array}{r} 10 \\ +\ 5 \\ \hline \end{array}$ | $\begin{array}{r} 14 \\ -\ 9 \\ \hline \end{array}$ | $\begin{array}{r} 13 \\ +\ 6 \\ \hline \end{array}$ | $\begin{array}{r} 14 \\ -\ 0 \\ \hline \end{array}$ | $\begin{array}{r} 12 \\ +\ 4 \\ \hline \end{array}$ | $\begin{array}{r} 9 \\ -\ 4 \\ \hline \end{array}$ | $\begin{array}{r} 20 \\ +\ 10 \\ \hline \end{array}$ | $\begin{array}{r} 60 \\ +\ 10 \\ \hline \end{array}$ |

○○○○

Day 1

1. Write the number that makes the number sentence true.

    _____ – 7 = 7

2. 14 + 40 = _____

    36 + 20 = _____

3. 80 – 40 = _____

    90 – 10 = _____

Day 2

1. Ava had 10 board games. Blane had 6 board games. Christopher had 4 board games. How many board games did they have altogether?

    _____ board games

2. Darius swam 7 laps in the lake in the morning. He swam 4 more laps after lunch. He took a break and then swam 2 more laps. How many laps did Darius swim in all?

    _____ laps

Day 3

1. Write the time shown on the clock.

    _____

2. What do you do at this time of the day?

    _____

Day 4

1. Color the circles. Circle the spheres.

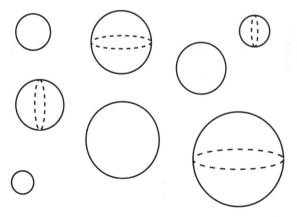

2. How many sides does a sphere have?

    _____

---

1. Look at the tally chart. Which month had the most sunny days?

Sunny Days		
June	July	August
卌 卌 |||	卌 卌	卌 |||

_____ had the most sunny days.

2. 80 – 10 = _____

   60 – 50 = _____

   40 – 10 = _____

3. Tavaris is reading a comic book. It has 20 pages. He read 10 pages. How many pages does Tavaris have left to read?

   _____ pages

4. Write the time shown on the clock.

   _____

5. Draw a picture using circles.

6. How many corners does a circle have?

   _____

 What is the most important thing you have learned in math this year? Why is it important?

Fluency Blast

Practice the math facts.

19	14	8	5	9	15	17	19	16	70
+ 1	− 1	+ 8	− 5	+ 9	− 1	+ 1	− 1	+ 1	+ 10

○○○○

Day 1

1. 17 − 3 = 3 + _____

2. Write the number that is 10 more than the number shown.

    74 _____

3. Write the number that makes the number sentence true.

    70 + _____ = 80

Day 2

1. Owen buys 16 hot dogs at the ball game. He gives away 8 hot dogs. How many hot dogs does Owen have left?

    _____ hot dogs

2. Emma, Felicia, and Ginny have 5 pet gerbils each. How many gerbils do the girls have altogether?

    _____ gerbils

Day 3

1. Write the time shown on the clock.

    _____

2. What time do you eat dinner?

    _____

Day 4

1. Use a trapezoid and a triangle to make a new shape.

2. How many sides does it have? _____

3. How many corners does it have? _____

1. Write the number that is 10 more than the number shown.

72 _____

Write the number that is 10 less than the number shown.

_____ 99

2. 6 + 10 + 10 = _____

13 + _____ = 53

3. Jordan read 17 pages of his textbook last night. He read 3 more pages this morning. When he got to school, he read 4 more pages. How many pages did Jordan read in all?

_____ pages

4. Write the time shown on the clock.

_____

5. Write the number that makes the number sentence true.

20 + _____ = 30

6. Draw two half circles to make a new shape. What is the name of the new shape? _____

 What is the one thing you are most proud of learning in math this year?

CD-104971 • © Carson-Dellosa

Fluency Blast

Practice the math facts.

12	18	15	14	4	13	12	9	10	6
+ 4	− 9	+ 5	− 9	+ 7	− 0	+ 2	− 8	+ 10	+ 6

○ ○ ○ ○

Day 1

1. 66 + 20 = _____

2.   13   27
      + 3   + 3

3.   69   22
      + 4   + 7

Day 2

1. Lila has 13 dice in her pocket. There are 9 white dice. The rest of the dice are pink. How many dice are pink?

_____ dice

2. Tarika invites 20 friends to her party. But, 2 of her friends cannot come to the party. How many friends are able to come to Tarika's party?

_____ friends

Day 3

1. Write the time shown on the clock.

_____

2. What do you do at this time of the day?

_____

Day 4

1. Color the triangles. Circle the cones.

2. Circle the defining attribute of a cone.

A. It has 1 face.

B. It looks like a party hat.

1.
```
   ¹
   37          58
 +  3        +  5
             63
```
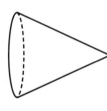
4 0

2.
```
   ¹
   12           9
 + 8         + 9
 20           18
```

3. Zack finds 12 pinecones. Chang gives him 10 more pinecones. Zack finds 1 more pinecone in the park. How many pinecones does Zack have in all?

12 + 10 + 1 23

_____ pinecones

4. Write the time shown on the clock.

9:30 _____

5. Write the name of the shape.

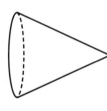

cone
_____

6. Circle the 2-D shape.

A. cone   B. (triangle)

 What is one math goal you have for next year? Why?

aDgin nombrs

1 2 3 4 5 6 7 8 9 10 11 12 13 14 15 16 17 18 19

Answer Key

Page 9
Day 1: 1. 23; 2. 5; 3. 7, 12, 6; **Day 2:** 1. 3, 2, 5; 2. 6, 3, 9; 3. 4, 4, 8; **Day 3:** 1. 6:00; 2. A; **Day 4:** 1. A; 2. 4; 3. A

Page 10
1. 5; 2. 25; 3. 4, 2, 6; 4. 9:00; 5. rectangle; 6. 4; Check students' work.

Page 11
Day 1: 1. 17; 2. 7; 3. 1, 4, 3; **Day 2:** 1. 4, 4, 8; 2. 6, 3, 9; **Day 3:** 1. 8:00; 2. B; **Day 4:** 1. B; 2. 0; 3. A

Page 12
1. 9; 2. 8; 3. 6, 2, 8; 4. 3:00; 5. circle; 6. 9, 11, 10

Page 13
Day 1: 1. 9; 2. 5; 3. true; **Day 2:** 1. 2, 1, 3; 2. 2, 3, 5; **Day 3:** 1. 9:00; 2. A; **Day 4:** 1. Check students' work. 2. 4; 3. Check students' work.

Page 14
1. 12; 2. 14; 3. 11, 9, 20; 4. 5:00; 5. square; 6. Check students' work.

Page 15
Day 1: 1. 10; 2. 5; 3. true; **Day 2:** 1. 3, 4, 7; 2. 10, 7, 17; **Day 3:** 1. 7:00; 2. A; **Day 4:** 1. Check students' work. 2. 3; 3. Check students' work.

Page 16
1. 10; 2. 14; 3. 3, 1, 4; 4. 11:00; 5. triangle; 6. A

Page 17
Day 1: 1. 6; 2. 17, 19, 11; **Day 2:** 1. 4, 3, 7; 2. 4, 10, 14; **Day 3:** 1. Check students' work. 2. A; **Day 4:** 1. B; 2. 4; 3. 4

Page 18
1. 6; 2. Check students' work. 3. 2, 2, 4; 4. 10:00; 5. triangle; 6. Answers will vary.

Page 19
Day 1: 1. 6; 2. 7; 3. 1, 4, 3; **Day 2:** 1. 1, 2, 1, 4; 2. 3, 4, 2, 9; **Day 3:** 1. 3:00; 2. A; **Day 4:** 1. A; 2. Answers will vary but may include that they have round edges and no corners or sides.

Page 20
1. 15; 2. false; 3. 7, 12, 19; 4–5. Check students' work. 6. Answers will vary.

Page 21
Day 1: 1. 15; 2. 3, 1, 2; 3. false; **Day 2:** 1. 1, 6, 7; 2. 4, 7, 11; **Day 3:** 1. 10:30; 2. A; **Day 4:** 1. Check students' work. 2. 1; 3. Check students' work.

Page 22
1. 18; 2. 20; 3. 4, 2, 2; 4. 2; 5. A; 6. B

Answer Key

Page 23
Day 1: 1. 10, 6, 12; 2. 19; 3. 6, 14, 1; **Day 2:** 1. 2, 1, 3; 2. 3, 2, 9, 14; **Day 3:** 1. 8:30; 2. B;
Day 4: 1. A; 2. 2; 3. Check students' work.

Page 24
1. 11, 3, 9; 2. 12; 3. 4, 3, 1; 4. 2:30; 5. cylinder; 6. circle

Page 25
Day 1: 1. 17; 2. 18; 3. >, <, >; **Day 2:** 1. 2, 2, 4; 2. 2, 5, 7; **Day 3:** 1. 11:30; 2. B; **Day 4:** 1. Check students' work. 2–3. Answers will vary.

Page 26
1. 17, 1, 9; 2. 14; 3. 4, 1, 3; 4. Check students' work. 5. >, =, <; 6. Check students' work. Answers will vary.

Page 27
Day 1: 1. 10; 2. 13; 3. <, <, >; **Day 2:** 1. 10, 9, 19; 2. 13, 5, 18; **Day 3:** 1. Check students' work. 2. A; **Day 4:** 1. B; 2. Answers will vary.

Page 28
1. 16; 2. 18; 3. 6, 5, 11; 4. Check students' work. 5. cube; 6. A

Page 29
Day 1: 1. 6, 1, 5; 2. 13; 3. <, <, =; **Day 2:** 1. 6, 2, 4; 2. 8, 2, 6; **Day 3:** 1. Check students' work. 2. B; **Day 4:** 1. B; 2. 0; 3. Check students' work.

Page 30
1. 4, 4, 8; 2. =, <, >; 3. 12, 1, 11; 4. Check students' work. 5. sphere; 6. 0

Page 31
Day 1: 1. 13; 2. <, >, <; **Day 2:** 1. 16, 6, 10; 2. 3, 1, 2; **Day 3:** 1. Check students' work. 2. B;
Day 4: 1. B; 2. 4; 3. Check students' work.

Page 32
1. 15; 2. >, <, =; 3. 15, 4, 11; 4. 3:00; 5. square; 6. 4; Check students' work.

Page 33
Day 1: 1. 9, 11; 2. false; 3. Check students' work. **Day 2:** 1. 4, 2, 6; 2. 1, 4, 5;
Day 3: 1. Check students' work. 2. Answers will vary. **Day 4:** 1. A; 2. 6; 3. Check students' work.

Page 34
1. Check students' work. 2. 18; 3. 9, 3, 6; 4–5. Check students' work. 6. 6

Page 35
Day 1: 1. 12, 3, 9; 2. seven, ten; **Day 2:** 1. 5, 6, 11; 2. 3, 7, 10; **Day 3:** 1. Check students' work. 2. B; **Day 4:** 1. Check students' work. 2. Answers will vary.

Page 36
1. Check students' work. 2. 13; 3. true; 4. Check students' work. 5. Answers will vary. Check students' work. 6. X: rectangle

CD-104971 • © Carson-Dellosa

Answer Key

Page 37
Day 1: 1. true; 2. 14; 3. Check students' work.
Day 2: 1. 17, 4, 13; 2. 12, 2, 10;
Day 3: 1. Check students' work. 2. B;
Day 4: 1. Check students' work. 2. 4;
3. Answers will vary but may include that it has one side that is longer than the other.

Page 38
1. 16, 10; 2. 18; 3. 10, 6, 16; 4–6. Check students' work.

Page 39
Day 1: 1. true; 2. 16; 3. 7; **Day 2:** 1. 12, 9, 3;
2. 12, 4, 16; **Day 3:** 1. 6; 2. Answers will vary.
Day 4: 1. Check students' work. 2. Answers will vary.

Page 40
1. Check students' work. 2. 20; 3. 15, 10, 5;
4. 4; 5. Check students' work. A; 6. Check students' work.

Page 41
Day 1: 1. 10, 11; 2. true; 3. 20, 30;
Day 2: 1. 3, 4, 7; 2. 12, 4, 16; **Day 3:** 1. 9;
2. Answers will vary. **Day 4:** 1. no; Answers will vary. 2. Check students' work.

Page 42
1. true; 2. 40, 20, 20; 3. 11, 3, 14; 4. 2, 1, 3;
5. rectangle; 6. 4

Page 43
Day 1: 1. true; 2. 20; 3. 1, 1; **Day 2:** 1. 7, 9, 16;
2. 8, 4, 12; **Day 3:** 1. 3, 2, 1; 2. A;
Day 4: 1. Check students' work. 2. 2; 3. A

Page 44
1. 16; 2. false; 3. 1, 5; 4. 1, 3, 2; 5. cylinder;
6. Check students' work.

Page 45
Day 1: 1. 14; 2. 0; 3. 1, 9; **Day 2:** 1. 15, 9, 6;
2. 15, 3, 12; **Day 3:** 1. 1, 2, 3; 2. B;
Day 4: 1. Check students' work. 2. cone;
3. 4, 4

Page 46
1. 17; 2. Answers will vary. Check students' work. 3. 1, 3; 4. 7; 5. cone; 6. Answers will vary.

Page 47
Day 1: 1. 18, 11; 2. 1, 6; 3. 30, 36;
Day 2: 1. 13; 2. 14; **Day 3:** 1. 5; 2. A;
Day 4: 1. Check students' work. 2. Answers will vary.

Page 48
1. 70; 2. Check students' work. 3. 5; 4. 1, 3, 2;
5. cube; 6. 6

Page 49
Day 1: 1. 1; 2. 3; 3. 1, 0; **Day 2:** 1. 3; 2. 6;
Day 3: 1. 3, 1, 2; 2. B; **Day 4:** 1. A; 2. 4; 3. 4

Answer Key

Page 50
1. 11; 2. 3, 8; 3. 1, 7; 4. 2, 3, 1; 5. A; 6. 0

Page 51
Day 1: 1. 18, 20; 2. 10, 30; **Day 2:** 1. 18; 2. 20; **Day 3:** 1, 2, 3; **Day 4:** 1. Check students' work. triangle; 2. 3; 3. Check students' work.

Page 52
1. 20, 50; 2. 20; 3. 18; 4. 8; 5. triangle; 6. Answers will vary.

Page 53
Day 1: 1. 4; 2. 18; 3. 6; **Day 2:** 1. 17; 2. 14; **Day 3:** 1. 10; 2. B; **Day 4:** 1. Check students' work. rectangle; 2. A

Page 54
1. 14, 2, 12, 3; 2. 11, 4, 10; 3. 4; 4. 3, 1, 2; 5. rectangle; 6. Answers will vary.

Page 55
Day 1: 1. 19, 19; 2. 49, 40; 3. 8; **Day 2:** 1. 10; 2. 6; **Day 3:** 1. 1, 2, 3; 2. A; **Day 4:** 1. Check students' work. square; 2. 4; 3. Check students' work.

Page 56
1. 16, 24; 2. true; 3. 23; 4. 3, 1, 2; 5. Check students' work. 6. Answers will vary.

Page 57
Day 1: 1. Check students' work. 2. 5; 3. 59; **Day 2:** 1. 12; 2. 18; **Day 3:** 1. 2, 3, 1; 2. A; **Day 4:** Check students' work.

Page 58
1. Check students' work. 2. 7, 12; 3. 38, 78; 4. 2, 3, 1; 5. Answers will vary. 6. Check students' work.

Page 59
Day 1: 1. 18, 12; 2. 29, 42, 54; **Day 2:** 1. 20; 2. 14; **Day 3:** 1. 2, 3, 1; 2. A; **Day 4:** 1. Check students' work. 2. A

Page 60
1. 12; 2. 2, 1; 3. 3; 4. 6; 5. cube; 6. Check students' work.

Page 61
Day 1: 1. >; 2. 6; 3. 96; **Day 2:** 1. 3; 2. 17; **Day 3:** 1. 4; 2. B; **Day 4:** 1. Check students' work. 2. B

Page 62
1. =, >; 2. 16, 73; 3. 1, 5; 4. 9; 5. Check students' work. 6. Answers will vary.

Page 63
Day 1: 1. 2, 8; 2. <; 3. 60; **Day 2:** 1. 36; 2. 23; **Day 3:** 1. 7; 2. A; **Day 4:** 1. Check students' work. 2. B

CD-104971 • © Carson-Dellosa

Answer Key

Page 64
1. 1, 9; 2. <, =; 3. 25, 20; 4. 3:00; 5. Check students' work. B; 6. 2

Page 65
Day 1: 1. <, >; 2. 42; 3. 98; **Day 2:** 1. 6; 2. 13; **Day 3:** 1. 8; 2. B; **Day 4:** 1. Check students' work. 2. A

Page 66
1. >, <; 2. 71, 5; 3. 6; 4. 5; 5. pentagon; 6. Answers will vary.

Page 67
Day 1: 1. 69, 47; 2. 3, 0; 3. 65; **Day 2:** 1. 17; 2. 13; **Day 3:** 1. 8:30; 2. B; **Day 4:** 1. Check students' work. 2. Answers will vary.

Page 68
1. 6, 0; 2. 92, 72; 3. 11; 4. 2:30; 5. triangle; 6. Answers will vary.

Page 69
Day 1: 1. >; 2. 29; 3. 25; **Day 2:** 1. 7; 2. 20; **Day 3:** 1. 7:30; 2. A; **Day 4:** 1. B; 2. 1; 3. Check students' work.

Page 70
1. 33, 78; 2. >, <; 3. 3; 4. 11:00; 5. half circle; 6. A

Page 71
Day 1: 1. 50, 79; 2. 8, 0; 3. 40, 30; **Day 2:** 1. 4; 2. 12; **Day 3:** 1. 2:00; 2. A; **Day 4:** 1. Check students' work. 2. 4; 3. Check students' work.

Page 72
1. 4, 0; 2. 55, 39; 3. <, =; 4. 5:30; 5. Check students' work. 6. 4

Page 73
Day 1: 1. 72; 2. >; 3. 51; **Day 2:** 1. 7; 2. 21; **Day 3:** 1. 2; **Day 4:** 1. Check students' work. 2. 3; 3. Check students' work.

Page 74
1. 88, 44; 2. 9, 0; 3. 9; 4. 5; 5–6. Answers will vary.

Page 75
Day 1: 1. 5, 0; 2. 75, 58; 3. 60, 30; **Day 2:** 1. 35; 2. 10; **Day 3:** 1. 4; **Day 4:** 1. Answers will vary. 2. B

Page 76
1. brown; 2. 95, 71; 3. 18; 4. 7, 3; 5. Answers will vary. 6. Check students' work.

Page 77
Day 1: 1. 3, 5; 2. >; 3. 73; **Day 2:** 1. 2; 2. 4; **Day 3:** 1. 3:30; 2. Answers will vary. **Day 4:** 1. Check students' work. 2. A

Answer Key

Page 78
1. 53, 54; 2. 1, 1; 3. 18; 4. 7:30; 5. balloon, tennis ball; 6. Answers will vary.

Page 79
Day 1: 1. =; 2. 5; 3. 59, 49; **Day 2:** 1. 7; 2. 28; **Day 3:** 1. 11:00; 2. Answers will vary. **Day 4:** 1–2. Check students' work.

Page 80
1. >, <; 2. 11; 3. 11; 4. 3:00; 5. Check students' work. 6. B

Page 81
Day 1: 1. 3; 2. 10; 3. 92, 35; **Day 2:** 1. 4; 2. 12; **Day 3:** 1. soccer; 2. baseball; **Day 4:** 1. Check students' work. 2. 4

Page 82
1. Lynn; 2. 16; 3. 10; 4. 10:30; 5. Check students' work. 6. Answers will vary.

Page 83
Day 1: 1. 14; 2. 54, 56; 3. 40, 80; **Day 2:** 1. 20; 2. 13; **Day 3:** 1. 11:30; 2. Answers will vary. **Day 4:** 1. Check students' work. 2. 0

Page 84
1. June; 2. 70, 10, 30; 3. 10; 4. 1:30; 5. Answers will vary. 6. 0

Page 85
Day 1: 1. 11; 2. 84; 3. 10; **Day 2:** 1. 8; 2. 15; **Day 3:** 1. 6:30; 2. Answers will vary. **Day 4:** 1–3. Answers will vary.

Page 86
1. 82, 89; 2. 26, 40; 3. 24; 4. 5:30; 5. 10; 6. Check students' work. circle

Page 87
Day 1: 1. 86; 2. 16, 30; 3. 73, 29; **Day 2:** 1. 4; 2. 18; **Day 3:** 1. 2:30; 2. Answers will vary. **Day 4:** 1. Check students' work. 2. A

Page 88
1. 40, 63; 2. 20, 18; 3. 23; 4. 9:30; 5. cone; 6. B

CD-104971 • © Carson-Dellosa

Notes